KNOW THAT YOU KNOW

What 1 John Tells Us about
ASSURANCE of SALVATION

PAUL SCH

First published in 2015 by Striving Together Publications, a ministry
of Lancaster Baptist Church, Lancaster, CA 93535. Striving Together
Publications is committed to providing tried, trusted, and proven
resources that will further equip local churches to carry out the
Great Commission. Your comments and suggestions are valued.

Striving Together Publications
4020 E. Lancaster Blvd.
Lancaster, CA 93535
800.201.7748
strivingtogether.com

Cover design by Matt Leckron
Layout by Craig Parker

The author and publication team have put forth every effort to give proper
credit to quotes and thoughts that are not original with the author. It is not
our intent to claim originality with any quote or thought that could not
readily be tied to an original source.

ISBN 978-1-59894-293-4
Printed in the United States of America

Contents

Introduction

An actor once said, "A man is not old until regrets take the place of dreams."[1] But for the Christian, it may well sound like this: A man is not old until regrets take the place of the will of God.

As an evangelist, I frequently hear the sad stories of people who wish they could have another chance at the will of God. They lament living for self, wealth, business, or pleasure instead of making their life count for God, and when they arrive at the precipice of eternity, they long for a mulligan. There is not much comfort for wasted days of regret.

Pastor John had no such contrition. As the book of 1 John opens, we can imagine the ninety-year-old pastor pulling up to his desk, lighting a candle, dipping his pen in the ink, and writing to the beloved church members in his home city of Ephesus.[2] He is thinking of the churches he has encouraged throughout the land that is known in our modern day as Turkey. It only seems that every other verse in 1 John finds this pastor writing to his "brethren" and his "little children."

Six decades had softened this mighty man of God. There was a day when Jesus hung the nickname Boanerges on him, but for this "son of thunder" the clap had quieted. He may have often remembered the day a welcoming committee in a Samaritan village did not properly roll out the red carpet for Jesus, so he asked, "Lord, wilt thou that we command fire to come down from heaven, and consume them, even as Elias did" (Luke 9:54)? The imprecations were now few and far between. Sixty years of service will invariably add "temperance…patience…(and) godliness" (2 Peter 1:6).

Though the years of servanthood made John patient with people, it would be a mistake to assume the fire was out. One of his disciples who pastored thirty miles away in Smyrna was Polycarp. He told of the day Pastor John entered an Ephesian bathhouse only to discover the heretic Cerinthus inside. John rushed out of the house crying, "Let us flee lest the bath fall in, as long as Cerinthus, that enemy of the truth, is within."[3]

So the disciple "whom Jesus loved" (John 13:23) had become the disciple who loved Jesus' children, and as the ninth decade of the first century rolled around, he was a burdened pastor. A spiritual crisis was brewing as Satan and his forces were fully engaged. From the outside, false teachers were rising by the day attacking the person of Christ. There was no apology from Pastor John as he labels them "antichrists" (1 John 2:18).

Others who once were trusted members of the Ephesian church had left proving "they were not of us" (1 John 2:19). They did not leave silently. Instead, they invested their lives in attempting to "seduce" (1 John 2:26) the members that remained. The words of Christ still rang in John's ears: "For there shall arise false Christs, and false prophets, and shall shew great signs and wonders; insomuch that, if it were possible, they shall deceive the very elect" (Matthew 24:24). "Christianity was not in danger of being destroyed; it was in danger of being changed. The attempt was being made to improve it, give it intellectual respectability, and let it speak in the terms of the popular philosophy."[4]

The attacks were not only from without but also within. Too many people that Pastor John invested his life in had succumbed to the temptations of the world. Some had "left (their) first love" (Revelation 2:4), some tolerated false doctrine (Revelation 2:15), some were dying on the vine (Revelation 3:1), and some were "lukewarm" (Revelation 3:16).

John was in a unique position to help them. When he preached, he did not rely on the theories of experts or the guesses of theologians. He declared,

"That which was from the beginning, which we have heard, which we have seen with our eyes, which we have looked upon, and our hands have handled, of the Word of life" (1 John 1:1). Others heard about Jesus, read about Jesus, and studied about Jesus, but John could say, "I heard Him. I saw Him. I touched Him. I know Him!"

So the old pastor pulls himself up to the desk with a job before him. The Spirit of God will speak the words, he will do the writing, and God will see to it that the words do not "return...void" (Isaiah 55:11). With so many problems and so many needs, it would be hard to know where to start. How do you help a church full of diverse issues? How do you stop the spread of error? How do you strengthen a church of people under attack?

A ninety-year-old pastor knows he has to go back to the basics. No one in the church will be able to stand unless they get it settled once and for all. It becomes the underlying theme in the book of 1 John, and it is the foundation for every Christian life.

"And hereby we do know that we know him" (1 John 2:3). We have to be sure. We have to have it settled and certain. We have to live without doubt.

We have to know that we know!

Chapter One

THE SECRET BATTLE

Who could have known? Certainly not the multitudes that listened to John the Baptist (not the same man as Pastor John) preach "Repent ye: for the kingdom of heaven is at hand" (Matthew 3:2).

Certainly not the religious leaders who chafed when he exposed them with these words: "O generation of vipers, who hath warned you to flee from the wrath to come?" (Matthew 3:7).

Certainly not the godly man waiting for the Messiah who rejoiced as he watched the preacher prepare "the way of the Lord" (Matthew 3:3).

Certainly not the Old Testament student who recognized that "Elias (Elijah) is come already" (Matthew 17:12), fulfilling the prophecy of Malachi.

It would have been impossible to know. After all, his life was the epitome of a righteous man. He was known to fast and pray. He lived a spartan lifestyle exhibiting a rejection of the world and a complete submission to God. To say that his clothing was unpretentious would be a massive understatement. He was so holy and pious that for a while, the crowds mused whether he was the Messiah himself.

But John the Baptist had a dark secret. It may have been hidden in the depths of his soul for the longest time, yet one day it surfaced. Imprisoned and facing death in a mountain fortress called Machaerus, it emerged when he told his disciples to find Jesus and ask, "Art thou he that should come, or do we look for another?" (Matthew 11:3) When they found the Son of God, Jesus responded, "Go and shew John again those things which ye do hear and see" (Matthew 11:4).

Did you notice the little word *"again?"* It appears this wasn't the first time Jesus dealt with the issue. It is wonderful to note that Jesus does not condemn John nor rebuke him, but in tender mercy He patiently helps him one more time.

John the Baptist battled doubt.

Churches are replete with members who fight a similar secret battle. Outwardly they boldly testify, *"Blessed assurance, Jesus is mine,"* but there is a dark secret on the inside. They will walk into a church-house with tithe in their pocket, a Bible under the arm, and a word of encouragement on their lips, yet in a world of which no one else knows, they are spiritually tormented. They are impossible to recognize for they look, walk, talk, dress, behave, and sing like Christians are supposed to; but it only covers a torturous war that plagues them constantly. They cannot speak about it; they are ashamed to admit it; but it is a real battle.

They don't know that they know.

If we had a roll call of those who fight this war, we would be flabbergasted. The list would contain deacons and Sunday School teachers and bus workers and choir members and youth workers. It would include Bible College professors and missionaries and evangelists and pastors. If we knew some of the names on the list we would be stunned, thinking it impossible that such esteemed, godly servants of Christ struggle so.

At times, the skirmish seems to dissipate, then the pastor preaches on the return of Christ in the clouds, and they fret they will be left behind. An evangelist preaches a fiery message on judgment, and they spend the night in abject fear they are going to die and suffer in Hell. They have walked down the aisle and wept at an altar. They have prayed the "sinners' prayer" a thousand times just to "make sure." They have scheduled counseling sessions with their pastor, and for a while, it seems that all is well. Then the nightmare returns, and it starts all over again. So this time they pray and "really mean it." Then they pray again and "really, really mean it." Then they pray again and "really, really, really mean it."

But when the dust settles, they don't *know that they know.* It is impossible to live the Christian life God desires for us until we absolutely *know that we know.*

So it is time for the old pastor to roll up his sleeves and get to work. Before the Christians in Ephesus could confront the false teachers, the doubts must be removed from their own souls. Via letter, Pastor John steps in the pulpit and preaches, "These things have I written unto you that believe on the name of the Son of God; that ye may know that ye have eternal life" (1 John 5:13). He knows his beloved children are going nowhere until they get it settled for good. Waffling Christians fretting over the issue of their salvation are easy pickings for fiery darts of the wicked one.

Years ago there lived a believer who was not well-educated, but had a deep assurance of his salvation. Everyone called him Old Pete. One day while talking with a pastor, he said, "If God should take me to the very mouth of Hell and say to me, 'In you go, Pete; here's where you belong,' I would say to Him, 'That's true, Lord, I do belong there. But if you make me go to Hell, Your dear Son Jesus Christ must go with me! He and I are now one, and we cannot be separated anymore.'"[5]

How many Christians would love to carry that level of assurance! It is the kind of boldness and belief the Saviour wants His children to possess; the courage and confidence the Bible is able to impart. Pastor John would not let one more fall without a fight. He is going to spend his days building a church of people strong in God's Word ready to confront the foe.

He wants them to *know that they know.*

Chapter Two

CLAIM2BES

Two ducks and a rather egotistical frog developed a friendship. When their pond dried up, the ducks knew they could easily fly to another location, but what of their friend the frog? Finally they decided to fly with a stick between their two bills and the frog hanging onto the stick by his mouth. All went well until a farmer looked up and saw them in the sky. "What a clever idea," said the man. "I wonder who thought of that?"

"I did," said the frog.[6]

As humans, we have developed a plethora of ways to get ourselves into trouble, but none are so potent or rapid as our speech. We create family, business, and interpersonal disasters with our words, and then have the audacity to think we can talk our way out of the problems we have just spoken into existence. As James observed, "Even so the tongue is a little member, and boasteth great things. Behold, how great a matter a little fire kindleth!…the tongue can no man tame; it is an unruly evil, full of deadly poison" (James 3:5, 8).

For the many calamities that our words produce, a potentially damning result is exposed in the doubting church member. Religious people have a tendency to talk themselves into believing that they are right with God when they often are not. They convince themselves of their own righteousness and mistakenly assume that God will accept them on their terms.

This was such a vast problem in the Ephesian church that Pastor John dealt with it six times in 1 John—an astounding number for such a short book. He introduced the subject with words like this: "If we say" (1 John 1:6). The phrase *we say* (actually one word in Greek) means to make a claim; to make an announcement. Six times in the book of 1 John, the old man of God confronts a church member who has set himself up as the authority and is following the dictates of his own thinking. He is telling anyone that will listen (usually himself) that he is right with God because he says so. His claim to eternal life is his own thinking and his own logic.

I often converse with pastors who are frustrated with some regular church attendees. Every week they walk into the building and take their seat in the back of the auditorium. They never sing praises to Christ; they never give; and they never participate in the service. When the Word of God is preached, there is a glazed look over their face with no signs of comprehension. Their life demonstrates no conviction of sin; they exhibit no Biblical characteristics of the Christian. When I ask the preacher if they are saved, he can only shrug his shoulders and say, "They claim to be."

They "claim to be" saved. I call them "claim2bes." Baptist churches have a host of onlookers who do not manifest Christianity with their lives, they do not get victory over sin, and they have no desire to serve God. Yet they are convinced they are going to Heaven because there was a religious experience in their life. They "claim to be" saved.

Pastor John had his claim2bes as well. He loved them enough to confront their thinking and insist they follow the Bible instead of human logic. If they were going to escape the wrath of Hell and be saved, they would have to come by the Word of God—not their personal claims.

It is instructive to see how Pastor John introduced the subject: "If we say that we have fellowship with him, and walk in darkness, we lie, and do not the truth" (1 John 1:6). Notice again the words *if we say*. John was including himself in the discussion. In effect, he was saying:

"A man could walk with Jesus for more than three years. He could be the disciple that Jesus loved, a pastor for six decades, a human author of five New

Testament books, but he will not talk his way into Heaven. I am no different than any other man or woman in this church. None of us will get to Heaven by our thinking, by our wisdom, or by our personal brand of religion."

The claim2bes in Ephesus sounded like many church members today:

- They claimed to have fellowship with Jesus, but walked in darkness (1 John 1:6).
- They claimed that they had no sin (1 John 1:8).
- They claimed that they had not sinned (1 John 1:10).
- They claimed to know Jesus, but they did not keep His commandments (1 John 2:4).
- They claimed to abide in Him (1 John 2:6).
- They claimed to be living in the light, but they hated their brother (1 John 2:9).

Pastor John was not impressed with their claims. Instead of taking their word for it, he responds with penetrating questions and cutting truth. Let's look at each of these:

> If we say that we have fellowship with him, and
> walk in darkness, we lie, and do not the truth:
> —1 JOHN 1:6

When a church attendee claimed to have fellowship with Jesus, John asked him why he was walking "in darkness...and (doing) not the truth." Instead of patting him on the back, the preacher went so far as to call such a person a liar, saying that a man who is constantly living in sin does not belong to God, irrespective of his affirmations.

> If we say that we have no sin, we deceive
> ourselves, and the truth is not in us....If we say
> that we have not sinned, we make him a liar, and
> his word is not in us.—1 JOHN 1:8, 10

Some of the claim2bes said they had no sin; others said they had not sinned. The statements are similar, but the nuance is important. The first is claiming he does not have a sin nature; the second is saying he had an event in his past life and has not sinned since.[7] Such a blasphemer is a consummate liar. He is lying to others; he is lying to himself; and most importantly, he is calling God a liar, mocking both the precious blood of Christ (verse 7) and the marvelous offer of God's mercy (verse 9).

It is said that Charles Spurgeon, the renown English pastor of yesteryear, was once confronted by a man who claimed to be without sin. Intrigued, the preacher invited him home for dinner. After hearing the claims through, Spurgeon picked up his glass of water and threw it in the man's face. Understandably, the visitor was highly indignant and expressed himself very forcefully to the preacher about his lack of courtesy, to which the wise man replied, "Ah, you see, the old man within you is not dead. He had simply fainted and could be revived with a glass of water!"[8]

Pastor John went on to explain that the claim2be was deceiving himself and "the truth is not in (him)." A deceived person is someone who is wandering aimlessly in his spiritual life with no one but himself to blame. He convinces himself that he is saved because of his life experience, and when one tells himself enough times that he is truly saved, pretty soon he accepts the lie.

> He that saith, I know him, and keepeth not his
> commandments, is a liar, and the truth is not in
> him.—1 JOHN 2:4

The claim2be says he knows Jesus, but "keepeth not his commandments." He may acknowledge the commands of God and recognize their importance. He may want the Ten Commandments posted in a courtroom and listed in a public school, but he does not personally keep them. He does not watch over them and guard them. They are not so vital that he exhibits a lifestyle demonstrating their value.

> He that saith he abideth in him ought himself
> also so to walk, even as he walked.—1 JOHN 2:6

The claim2be will tell everyone listening that "he abideth in him," but there is no desire to walk as Jesus did. To abide means "to continue, to remain in, to keep on,"[9] and it was a favorite phrase of Pastor John.[10] The abider will stand the test of time, a truth attested by the six decades John had remained faithful to Christ. The abider recognizes his obligation (note the word *ought*) will never end, and he will demonstrate that conviction by walking as Jesus did.

> He that saith he is in the light, and hateth his brother, is in darkness even until now.
> —1 JOHN 2:9

The claim2be says "he is in the light," but he hates his brother. He is saying with his tongue that he has a special enlightenment that comes from knowing Jesus, but his life exhibits a hatred for the brothers. There is no case in the New Testament where the word *brother* refers to all of humanity; in most cases, it refers to saved members of a local church.[11] The subject of the verse is an unsaved member of the church in Ephesus. He tells himself that he is in the light of Christ, but he is really "in darkness."

How tragic! A man or woman can carry a Bible under their arm, sing the praises of God, give to support missionaries, and still be lost. They convince themselves that they are saved, yet the basis of their salvation is their own ideas, beliefs, and, frankly, imagination. They are expecting to go to Heaven because of what they claim.

The claim2bes expose the greatest reason many church members battle the question of assurance. There is a basic question, yet it goes right to the heart of the matter:

What is the authority of my salvation?

When this kind of doubter gets to the bottom line, he will find that his claims are his authority. In essence, he is trying to talk his way into Heaven. If he claims loud enough, long enough, passionately enough, ultimately it should be enough.

Claim2bes point to the flyleaf of a Bible where a parent, a pastor, or a camp counselor wrote the date they were converted. They fondly remember walking an aisle at a great crusade where they experienced a moving emotional experience. They have prayed prayers, entered the waters of baptism, or submitted to religious sacraments, but in the quietness of the night, the doubt is gnawing at them and eating at their soul. They are trusting claims that come from their own desperate hearts which can never assure.

The claim2be is looking to the wrong source, and the problem only worsens.

They don't *know that they know*.

Chapter Three

THE TRUTH

The error of the claim2bes was their belief that truth lived in their minds. Pastor John did not waste a lot of ink before he exposed them: "If we say that we have fellowship with him, and walk in darkness, we lie, and *do not the truth*" (1 John 1:6). Then he added: "If we say that we have no sin, we deceive ourselves, and *the truth is not in us*" (1 John 1:8). In case they missed it, he went on: "He that saith, I know him, and keepeth not his commandments, is a liar, and *the truth is not in him*" (1 John 2:4).

If the church members wanted to *know that they know,* they needed convincing about this basic issue. They had to understand what truth was and then determine that truth alone will be the foundation for their faith. Certainly Pastor John would be qualified to help us with a simple but supremely seminal question: What is truth?

"Thy word is truth" (John 17:17). Nothing less than Scripture will suffice. If the church members in Ephesus wanted to experience the assurance of God they would have to go the Bible as the only authority. Parents are a special gift of God, but they are not the arbiters of eternal life. Pastors are a blessing of God, but they do not have an ability to peer into the human soul and render a verdict on the spiritual condition of a member. As 1 Samuel 16:7 says, "Man looketh on the outward appearance, but the LORD looketh on the heart." When it comes to a human entering Heaven, God gets the first, the last, and the only word.

Understanding that his members had to recognize the Bible as the ultimate authority of truth, Pastor John carefully builds the case. "If we say that we have no sin, we deceive ourselves, and the truth is not in us....If we say that we have not sinned, we make him a liar, and his word is not in us" (1 John 1:8, 10). Because the deceived man did not have the truth in him, he did not know the Bible, understand the Bible, nor mediate upon the Bible; and ultimately, the Word of God was not woven into the fabric of his life and thinking.

No wonder they had so many doubts! Their standard was human logic and reason, yet no human heart has ever understood the immense mind of God. Psalm 92:5 declares, "O LORD, how great are thy works! and thy thoughts are very deep."

Pastor John was not done: "And hereby we know that we are of the truth, and shall assure our hearts before him" (1 John 3:19). The word *assure* means "to convince the heart, to exhibit confidence and assurance in a situation which might otherwise cause dismay or fear."[12] This confidence is critical, for the Bible says our hearts need to be assured "before him." While some might battle their own conscience and reasoning, the far more relevant issue is the future event when we stand before God, and it is paramount that we "have boldness in the day of judgment" (1 John 4:17). The only hope of standing undaunted before God will come from the Bible. If we will be assured in the face of the coming judgment, we must be "of the truth."

When a person goes to the Bible, they go to the "record" of God (1 John 5:10) which is also called the "witness" of God. When they fill their lives with the Word of God, the truth is in them, and their personal faith will only grow stronger for "faith cometh by hearing, and hearing by the word of God" (Romans 10:17). When it runs its course, Pastor John tells us what it produces:

> He that believeth on the Son of God hath the witness in himself: he that believeth not God hath made him a liar; because he believeth not the record that God gave of his Son. And this is the record, that God hath given to us eternal life, and this life is in his Son. He that hath the Son hath life; and he that hath not the Son of God hath not life. These things have I written unto

you that believe on the name of the Son of God;
that ye may know that ye have eternal life, and
that ye may believe on the name of the Son of
God.—1 JOHN 5:10–13

It is impossible to believe in Christ and reject the
Bible. The only authority on the subject of eternal life
is the Word of God, and if a sinner does not accept
what God has stated, he cannot be saved. The Bible
tells us that eternal life is the gift of God. The Bible
tells us Jesus is life. The Bible tells us to believe on
His name.

God's record. God's witness. God's truth. God's
Word. When we are placing our confidence in His
perfect words, we are trusting the one who "cannot
lie" (Titus 1:2). Such a claim can never be made about
another human, nor can it be made about our own
hearts, but it certainly defines the character of God.

Pastor John made it personal for his church.
The Bible was written "unto you" so that "ye may
know that ye have eternal life." He was speaking
to individuals in the church that had believed "on
the name of the Son of God." Religion tends to deal

with people as a mass, but Bible Salvation is always a personal choice. Sinners are not saved as a group, a family, or a church. They are saved one by one.

Pastor John sent them to the written Word of God, informing them that the Bible was written so they could *know that they know*. In the book of 1 John there are different words used to describe knowledge. In this case, a knowledge is gained by instruction as opposed to a knowledge that we gain from life experience. Eternal life is "something that can be known apart from experience. It is known by believing God's testimony, not looking to one's works for assurance."[13]

Pastor John put eternal life in the present tense. He tells the people that if they have trusted the name of Christ for salvation they "have" eternal life. Eternal life does not start when a person dies and meets God; it begins the moment they are saved (1 John 5:12). When Pastor John stood in the pulpit on a Sunday morning, he was looking into faces of people who already possessed eternal life.

I heard of a little boy who was having doubts. At some point in a Sunday School class, he heard a teacher say that Satan was his enemy, so he figured the devil must be giving him the doubts. His teacher also told the class that the devil loved darkness. When the boy looked around his room, he noticed the darkest place was under his bed, so he concluded the devil must be there. He opened his Bible to John 3:16, shoved it under his bed, and said, "Here! Read it for yourself!"

Pastor John is telling us to "read it for ourselves." If a person desires to *know that he knows,* he must choose to let the Bible be the sole authority of salvation. He will not combine the Bible with the wisdom of his pastor, his parents, his counselors, his professors, his friends, his confidants, or any other frail human. The difference between Heaven or Hell for eternity is far too important an issue to depend on the opinions of man, so he will read it for himself.

Decades ago, in northeast India, there existed a tribe of headhunters known as the Hmars. Their tribe was one of the most feared in the land, famous for the human heads they hung over the doors of their bamboo huts. On one occasion they raided a tea plantation and claimed five *hundred* victims. The British commander, General Lord Roberts, came after the tribesmen in two military columns, managing to kill a few tribesmen, but most escaped into the jungle.

Back in Europe a chemist by the name of Watkin Roberts had been converted during the Welsh Revival. When he read Lord Robert's account of the Hmars pursuit, he believed God was leading him to get the Bible to that tribe. When he arrived at the border of the Hmar territory, however, the British authorities turned him away saying the area was too dangerous. Roberts managed to find a nearby tribe with a similar language and began to translate the Bible. When an English woman sent him a small gift of five pounds, he printed a few hundred copies of the Gospel of John and used a British runner to send a copy to each of the Hmar villages.

One of these copies was read before a Hmar chief. He was not able to understand what it meant to be "born again" as described in John 3, so he sent an invitation to Roberts to come and explain.

When Roberts showed the chief's invitation to the British official, the agent retorted, "That's an invitation to have your head lopped off. They'll make a celebration out of you." Despite the warnings, Roberts went to the tribe and patiently preached Christ to them.

Days later, the chief and four other Hmar men announced they wanted to make peace with the great God of the Bible by believing on Christ. One of the men, Chawanga Pudaite, became one of the first Hmar preachers traveling by canoe and foot through the territory preaching Christ. He was used of God to see multitudes saved and countless churches established in nearly every village as the gospel of Christ changed lives and communities. The headhunting became an activity of the past as did the drunkenness and fighting and fears.

When the British branded Roberts a troublemaker for his part in the transformation and ordered him to leave, the translation work was placed into the hands of Rochunga Pudaite, the preacher's son. The villagers sent him to a mission school and then to Bible schools in Scotland and America so he could do the translation work.

Over time, the Hmars became one of the most advanced ethnic groups in India. Today, at least ninety-five percent claim to be born again Christians, worshiping in over two hundred churches. Except for Mr. Roberts, the only missionary they have had is the Bible. With the Hmar population now up to 125,000, 85 percent can read and write—a phenomenal percentage. They have eighty-eight church-sponsored elementary schools, seven junior high schools, and four secondary high schools—one with an enrollment of about a thousand. They even have a hospital, staffed by skilled Hmar doctors and nurses.

The Hmars began taking the gospel to other tribes, starting hundreds of churches in different territories. As for Rochunga Pudaite, he is now head of an organization called *Bibles for the World*, which has already mailed millions of Bibles to postal addresses in scores of countries. He has a vision to mail at least one Bible to each of the one billion telephone addresses worldwide.

Pudaite said, "The Bible is the Book that reveals the mind of God, the heart of man, the way of salvation, and the blessedness of believers. It is the Book that tells us where we come from and where we are going. *It is the Book that set my people free.*"[14]

How right he is! It is the only book that sets the sinner free. It is the only book that explains how a wicked man can be made righteous before God. It is the only book that prepares a person for eternity.

It is the only book that will explain how people can *know that they know.*

Chapter Four

WHAT WE CAN KNOW

When the Golden Gate Bridge in San Francisco was in the early stages of construction, no safety devices were used, and twenty-three men fell to their deaths. For the last part of the project a large net which cost $100,000 was employed. At least ten men fell into it and were saved. But an interesting sidelight is the fact that twenty-five percent more work was accomplished when the men were assured of their safety.[15]

Pastor John understood the helplessness of the church member who did not have a "safety net." The doubt incessantly torments, creating an unsettled person unable to work for Christ. Until the heart is assured before God (1 John 3:19), there will never be a strong, confidant Christian prepared to step out in faith. When the heart is finally settled, the work that is accomplished for Christ is even greater.

The book of 1 John uses two different words to describe the knowledge a child of God must possess. One type of knowledge, discussed twenty-five times in 1 John, comes from a life of experience. Over time, our understanding increases, and we are able to perceive and grasp truths we may have previously missed. The second type of knowledge, mentioned fifteen times in 1 John, is a knowledge we gain from facts. Though the words are often used interchangeably, there is a distinction that is important to understand.

Assured Christians balance these two words. They have a habit of studying the Scriptures so they have an accurate "book knowledge" of Jesus, but they also determine to build a walk with God that allows them an "experiential knowledge." If that balance is out of kilter, the person will wind up being "too smart" or "too sensitive." Knowledge without experience produces a critical, arrogant Pharisee who knows about God but is not influenced by God, while experience without knowledge produces an unstable man who follows his emotional impulses.

Pastor John set out to build a people with the right balance. One can imagine the old preacher shaking his bony finger in the air and reminding the congregation, "You can know! God wants you to know!" Throughout the book of 1 John, he carefully spells out what the Christian needs to know:

We can "know that we know him" (1 John 2:3). Six decades earlier, John listened as Jesus prayed, "And this is life eternal, that they might know thee the only true God, and Jesus Christ, whom thou hast sent" (John 17:3). He never got over it. He does not stand before the church and demand, "*You* need to know him." Instead, he said "*we*" need to know him.

That means that we can know Jesus just like John knew Jesus. As a young boy, John knew Jesus as his cousin. As a man, he knew Jesus as the fisher of men. At Calvary, he knew Jesus as the Saviour of the world. But six decades later, he knew Jesus as the Lord of his life.

We tend to put Bible characters on a pedestal and suppose their intimate experience with God puts them in a different sphere. Not so. Pastor John tells Christians down through the ages there is no secret system in place. It is not enough to know facts and stories and songs about Jesus; we need to know Him for ourselves. The longer we walk with Him and the longer we learn of Him, the more we come to know Him.

So how do we know that we know Him? First John 2:3 gives a simple test: "And hereby we do know that we know him, if we keep his commandments." Our human logic and religious training would conclude that by keeping His commands we would learn to know Him, but Jesus reverses that thinking. When we know Him, obedience will follow as the natural outgrowth of salvation. Obedience is not the way to know Him; it is the proof that we already know Him.

We can know "it is the last time" (1 John 2:18). Like the Apostle Paul, John was looking for the "blessed hope" (Titus 2:13). He did not preach, "In two thousand years it will be the last time," but he reminded the members of the Ephesian church that they were living in the last times: "Little children, it is the last time: and as ye have heard that antichrist shall come, even now are there many antichrists; whereby we know that it is the last time" (1 John 2:18).

The "last time" began the moment Jesus ascended into Heaven with the promise "I will come again" (John 14:3). Like John, we are living at a stage in history where the return of Christ is but a "twinkling of an eye" away (1 Corinthians 15:52). Many are the scoffers who taunt, "Where is the promise of his coming? for since the fathers fell asleep, all things continue as they were from the beginning of the creation" (2 Peter 3:4). They are willingly ignorant of the fact that the Word of God will not be mocked, and that "one day is with the Lord as a thousand years, and a thousand years as one day" (2 Peter 3:8).

A child of God is expected to live with anticipation that Jesus may appear at any moment, and such an expectation produces someone who knows "when he shall appear, we shall be like him; for we shall see him as he is," as well as one who decides to purify "himself, even as he is pure" (1 John 3:2–3).

Many Christians have been caught up in the excitement of Bible prophecy. They are captivated by preachers who flagrantly disobey the Bible in setting dates for the return of Christ. They are fascinated by experts speculating as to who the Antichrist will be. Prophecy preaching is critically important, but its greatest purpose is served when it changes our present lives. We can almost hear Pastor John:

"Jesus is coming again! Are you ready? If you are not saved, your last opportunity will one day be gone. If you know the Lord, are you prepared to meet Him? Will He find us a pure church body that has forsaken the world and its attractions? If one day we will be like Him, then we should start practicing now. We have to make the personal choice to purify ourselves, because Jesus is pure—it is His character!"

We can know our Bible (1 John 2:20–21). "But ye have an unction from the Holy One, and ye know all things." As saved people, we have been given the Holy Spirit, a special gift from the Holy One, God the father, and what a gift He is![16]

An *unction* means "to assign a person to a task, with the implication of supernatural sanctions, blessing, and endowment."[17] When the Holy Spirit dwells in a saved person, He equips him to live the Christian life with a special enablement allowing the child of God to "know all things." Obviously, we do not become omniscient at the moment of salvation and possess the mind of God, but we do have every necessary tool to discern truth from error and to live victoriously. We have the capacity to know and comprehend everything necessary for the Christian life.

One might hear a church member ask Pastor John, "If the Spirit of God is in me and I have an unction, why do I struggle so?" His answer is powerful: "I have not written unto you because ye know not the truth, but because ye know it, and that no lie is of the truth."

The Holy Spirit enables every Christian to understand and obey the written Word of God. They don't need another authority in their lives. Every religion will offer a pope, a priest, a minister, a scholar, all of whom are generously given by the hierarchy to the common masses who evidently cannot make it without such experts. But God did not give us a seminary professor so we can understand the Bible; He gave us the Spirit of God. "But the anointing which ye have received of him abideth in you, and ye need not that any man teach you" (1 John 2:27).

The Spirit of God and the Word of God! That is all I need to know the "truth" (1 John 2:21). That is all I need to discern the errors of false religion (1 John 2:22). That is all I need to continue in the faith (1 John 2:24). That is all I need to abide in Him (1 John 2:27).

We can know who Jesus is (1 John 3:5). This would seem simple enough, yet the person of Christ is the dividing issue between truth and error. In John's day the false religions were waging a full assault against the Son of God. Docetism taught that Jesus did not have a literal body. Cerinthianism claimed that a divine spirit descended on Jesus at his baptism but departed at the cross. In our day, Mormons and Jehovah's Witnesses claim that Jesus is not eternal but a created being. The issue is always Jesus.

It would have been fascinating to hear Pastor John give his testimony. He could tell of growing up in the wealthy home of the fishing magnate Zebedee. He first enters the Scriptures as an ardent follower of John the Baptist, yet when John pointed him to Christ, he followed the Lamb of God. After a time, he went back to the fishing nets, but one day he was challenged to lay it all on the altar of sacrifice for Christ, and he never looked back. The rest of his life was dedicated to telling the world who Jesus is.

"And ye know that he was manifested to take away our sins; and in him is no sin." Pastor John continued to hammer the false doctrine of his day. He tells his church members that Jesus was *manifested*. In other words, though He already existed in eternity past because He is the eternal Christ, one day He was simply manifested (made visible) upon this earth. Jesus was never created, because He always was.

Like John the Baptist taught him, Pastor John told his church that Jesus came to "take away our sins." The verb *take away* pictures someone lifting a heavy load and taking it upon himself, which is precisely what Jesus did on the cross. The reason He is able to take away our sins (plural) is because in Him "is no sin" (singular). Sins are the acts that we commit; sinless is the permanent state of Jesus. He cannot commit sins because He is not a sinner.

How powerful and simple are the eighteen words in this verse that correct false teaching! Jesus is eternal. Jesus is not a created being. Jesus is begotten of God. Jesus is the bearer of our sins. Jesus never sinned. Jesus is unable to sin.

Strong Christians know who Jesus is. They don't care to know the Christ of religion, the Christ of Hollywood movies, or the Christ of the gospel singers, but they desire to know the Christ of the Bible.

Pastor John was not done. He wanted the church to know more about Jesus:

- That Jesus cleanses sinners (1 John 1:7).
- That Jesus is righteous (1 John 2:1).
- That Jesus is the Christ (1 John 2:22).
- That Jesus destroys the works of the devil (1 John 3:8).
- That Jesus was dwelling in them (1 John 3:24).
- That Jesus Christ is come in the flesh (1 John 4:2).
- That Jesus is the only begotten Son of God (1 John 4:9).
- That Jesus is the propitiation for our sins (1 John 4:10).
- That Jesus is the Saviour of the world (1 John 4:14).
- That Jesus came by water and by blood (1 John 5:6).
- That Jesus and God and the Holy Spirit are one (1 John 5:8).
- That eternal life is in Christ (1 John 5:11).
- That Jesus Christ is the true God (1 John 5:20).

One day I was giving the gospel to a Jehovah's Witness, she bitterly said, "You are not going to start quoting that John fellow, are you?" That "John fellow" invested his life in knowing Christ, and he took every opportunity to help others know Him as well. There is a very good reason that false religions run as fast as they can from a book like 1 John, for if people go to the book, they will know Christ. If they know Christ, they will flee false religion.

My daughter Becky used to work as a bank teller where she was exceptionally proficient at recognizing counterfeit dollars. I once asked her how she was trained to spot the phony bills. She told me they spent hours learning what the real bill looked like and felt like. Once she knew the real, it became easy to spot the fraud.

Pastor John did the same thing. False religions have always created their own christ, but the best way to spot the fraud is to know the real. He wanted the people to know all about Christ, and he wanted them to know Him personally.

We can know we are in His family (1 John 3:14). The local church is a wonderful creation of Christ. As Pastor John dealt with the "brethren" and "little children" in the assembly, he repeatedly reminded them of the importance of loving each other. "We know that we have passed from death unto life, because we love the brethren." Where else does such love exhibit itself?

Pastor John might well have used the church at Antioch as a sermon illustration. The first century world was divided over race and religion but God's people were different. It had as its leaders a diverse group, including Barnabas, who was a Jew from Cyprus; Simeon, who most likely was from Africa; Lucius, who was probably a Roman from Cyrene; Manaen, who was an aristocrat who had been raised with Herod the tetrarch; and Saul, who was a Jewish teacher from Tarsus (Acts 13:1).[18]

We live in a world that simply can't get along. We fight over race, wealth, status, and countless other issues, yet in the local church the items that divide the world are laid aside. The moment people cross the threshold of the meeting house, it no longer matters what their social level is or what the color of their skin may be. Yankee fans get along with Red

Sox fans; Cowboys fans with Redskins fans; Duke fans with Tarheel fans; Republicans and Democrats are now brothers and sisters. Often I am privileged to preach at churches near military bases where I am always amazed that rank matters from Monday through Saturday, but not on Sunday. Don't get me wrong; churches do have issues. No one is perfect, and since churches are made up of people, no church is perfect either. Yet, in Christ, we have the love of God to overcome cultural and natural divides. Pastor John included himself in the mix when he said, "Beloved, let us love one another." From pulpit to pew we are family.

John repeatedly tells his people that love is a mark of the child of God. We know that we are in His family because we love people that we could not have loved before we were saved. We do not have a false love full of empty words, but we love "in deed and in truth" (1 John 3:18). The love we demonstrate to our brothers and sisters shows the Bible and the Saviour residing in our hearts resulting in a love that is not temporary, but a love that keeps on loving.

When someone has a need, those who have "this world's good" (1 John 3:17) do whatever it takes to meet the need. Notice the word *good* is a singular word. It is not simply saying that rich people are taking care of poor people, but rather that everyone who "has it good" is doing their part. The healthy bear the burden of the sick. The hungry find a spot at the table from those who have the bread.

When the Bible says, "Beloved, let us love one another: for love is of God; and every one that loveth is born of God, and knoweth God" (1 John 4:7), it is evident that the love in the local church is produced by God and not humans. This love is not a response of an emotion but the result of a changed life. Only someone born again of God can be transformed into a man that loves the brothers.

In an 1918 publication by Ralph Waldo Trine titled *The Higher Powers of Mind and Spirit,* he relates the following anecdote: "Do you know that incident in connection with the little Scottish girl? She was trudging along, carrying as best she could a boy younger, but it seemed almost as big as she herself, when one remarked to her how heavy he must be for her to carry, when instantly came the reply: 'He's na heavy. He's mi brither.'"[19]

That's the local church. Nobody is too heavy. "He's my brother."

We can know our prayers are answered (1 John 5:14–15). This is the fourth time Pastor John reminds his people of the confidence they have in Christ, an assured boldness that strengthens the longer they are saved.[20] "And this is the confidence that we have in him, that, if we ask any thing according to his will, he heareth us: And if we know that he hear us, whatsoever we ask, we know that we have the petitions that we desired of him."

The religions of the world cannot bring such confidence. I have witnessed people bowing before ornate shrines in Malaysia offering incense and gifts to Buddhist idols. It may be a student with a big exam that day or a businessman seeking to seal a deal. It may be an older person in poor health or a mother wishing the best for her child, but the golden Buddha can never instill confidence. They enter the presence of a dead idol, they bow before a dead idol, they pray to a dead idol, and they walk away hoping against hope.

In Sicily, I watched scores of people crawl up ninety concrete steps on their knees to pray before a graven image depicting the Virgin Mary. When they reached the top of the stairs, their bloody knees testified to their devotion, but the altar of marble could never answer their prayers. Dead idols cannot hear. Their worshippers can only leave with no confidence.

When the child of God enters the closet of prayer, he is entering into the presence of the living God. When we pray according to His will and His Word, we know that He hears us. We are not trying to get Him to see things our way, nor are we trying to extract our wish list from Him. We are simply submitting our will to His desires and asking for those things that please Him. He is hearing us as we are praying. It is all in the present tense.

Praying is such a confidence builder that Pastor John uses the word *know* twice. "And if we *know* that he hear us, whatsoever we ask, we *know* that we have the petitions that we desired of him."

We know that we know!

What a wonderful Father! He is doing what a dead god is unable to do. He not only listens; He listens with favor.[21] He is going out of His way to pay attention.

Years ago, I was preaching a meeting in the mountains of western North Carolina. During the Sunday morning service, the pastor stood before the people and told them it was time to pray. All of the men stepped out of their seats, knelt at the front of the auditorium, and did something you don't see growing up in formal Connecticut. They prayed out loud all together at the same time. And the Lord heard every word.

He listens to the petitions of His people in all languages and nations. The cries of a villager in an African jungle are heard just like the cries of someone from the concrete jungle of Shanghai. A mariner out on the ocean waters is heard just like the godly invalid who cannot rise from a hospital bed. "But the LORD is the true God, he *is* the living God, and an everlasting king" (Jeremiah 10:10).

Notice the abridged list (there are other truths Pastor John wanted the church members to know) again:

- We know that we know Him.
- We know it is the last days.
- We know the Word of God.
- We know the Son of God.
- We know He answers prayer.

This is a list that matters to the child of God, but the unsaved world cares for none of these things. The lost man does not want to know Jesus. He does not care about the return of Christ. He finds the local church boring and finds it hard to spend sixty minutes a week within its walls. He does not want to pray.

When a man desires to know Christ and His Word, loves the brothers of the local church, reminds himself that Jesus is coming again, and works at building a prayer life, he has characteristics in his life that cannot be humanly produced. It may be possible to play the game for a period of time, but Pastor John constantly uses verbs in the present tense. The true child of God has a permanently changed life that is continually affecting the way he lives. He has been changed and is not going back.

When a man can look at his life and honestly see these desires, he begins to build the confidence that John wanted his church members to have. He is a changed man, and he knows those changes did not come from his own will. I love to hear the testimonies of people in local churches who have recently been saved. Often they will say something like this: "If you would have told me a year ago that I would be here to day, I would have said you were crazy."

Exactly. When a man is saved he is transformed by the Spirit of God. It is a work only God can do. When that work happens in a life, a man becomes confident.

He knows that he knows.

Chapter Five

QUESTIONS TO CONFIRM

As Pastor John patiently deals with his church members, he invites them to look to their own hearts. He joins the Apostle Paul: "Examine yourselves, whether ye be in the faith; prove your own selves. Know ye not your own selves, how that Jesus Christ is in you, except ye be reprobates?" (1 Corinthians 13:5). He wanted the members of the Ephesian church to know how normal Christians live, and then relate the issue to themselves.

Every church member should approach 1 John in the same manner. While it is unprofitable for someone to constantly question their salvation to the point of being spiritually paralyzed, there should be occasions where we take stock of our standing before God. A series of questions then can be asked from 1 John that we should use individually to "examine…prove… (and) know."

These questions can serve two purposes: First, a person may look at the issues raised in 1 John and discern they are not living as a Christian lives. Perhaps they are doubting their salvation because they are not truly saved. In such a case, it must be the Bible that brings conviction. Second, these issues and questions raised by John can easily confirm a person's salvation. These marks and distinctions may be imitated for a period of time, but if a person has a desire to live like a Christian, and they demonstrate that desire over a period of time, their life is producing spiritual results that are unnatural for a lost person.

If someone finds himself honestly answering "no" to these questions, there is a real problem. If someone finds himself honestly answering "yes," there is a great confirmation. This list is by no means the complete and only list of questions that may be asked from 1 John, so it is best to search the Scriptures and study 1 John in particular for yourself and make your own, but this is a solid start:

1. Do I love God's people?

Pastor John starts the book of 1 John with these words: "That which we have seen and heard declare we unto you, that ye also may have fellowship with us: and truly our fellowship *is* with the Father, and with his Son Jesus Christ" (1 John 1:3). In verse 7, he adds, "But if we walk in the light, as he is in the light, we have fellowship one with another, and the blood of Jesus Christ his Son cleanseth us from all sin."

In John's day, fellowship was a critical issue. Many in his church had been tossed out of their families, fired from their jobs, and paid a handsome price to follow Christ. Jewish Christians in the first century were often excommunicated from their synagogues becoming pariahs to the world.

To such individuals, the local church was not a mere social institution—it was their family. The New Testament word *fellowship* expressed that relationship. The word means an "association involving close mutual relations and involvement."[22] We tend to think of fellowship as enjoying a cup of coffee with someone and engaging in idle conversation about the weather, but they thought of fellowship as sharing their lives.

Their fellowship was centered on their Saviour. It did not matter how wealthy or how poor they were; it did not matter whether one was a Jew and another a Gentile. All that counted was the fact that God was their Father and Jesus their Saviour. Walking in the light of Christ produced a church of people that were fellowshipping as family, and whatever their differences may have been, they were united because of Jesus.

When someone is saved by the blood of Christ, they desire "fellowship one with another" in the local church. So we may well ask ourselves, "Do I desire the fellowship of the local church? Would I rather spend my time with God's people in the church or with the lost in the world? With whom am I more comfortable? Who is my crowd?"

When someone is born of God they desire to be with people that are also born of God. They love to hear others sing of Christ and talk of Him. When they are in the world, they are offended when God's name is profaned. They don't find filthy jokes funny. The sins that once dominated their lives are repulsive to them, and they don't want to be in a place where they are constantly reminded of the past life.

A lost person is just the opposite. He finds church and its members boring and dull. He doesn't like music that exalts Jesus. He can't wait to get out of the building and get back to his sin because his crowd is this lost world.

So who is our crowd? If we are naturally drawn to the saved, we are living a life that is unnatural for this world. If we are naturally drawn to the unsaved, we need to ask ourselves why this is so. Saved people want to fellowship with saved people. Does this describe our lives?

2. Am I comfortable with my sin?

Pastor John was on the war path against sin. Six decades of pastoring brought too many stories of ruined lives, so the passion in his heart is evident. Listen to him pleading with the Ephesian saints: "If we say that we have no sin, we deceive ourselves…if we confess our sins, he is faithful and just to forgive us our sins…if we say that we have not sinned, we make him a liar…these things write I unto you, that ye sin not… whosoever committeth sin transgresseth also the law… he that committeth sin is of the devil…whosoever is born of God doth not commit sin…he cannot sin, because he is born of God…all unrighteousness is sin: and there is a sin not unto death."

These verses have been misunderstood and misused through the years resulting in confused people. Some have taught that a Christian must be sinless and should they ever sin, they have lost their salvation. Pastor John obliterated that argument when he included himself in 1 John 1:8: "If we say that we have no sin, we deceive ourselves, and the truth is not in us." As long as we reside in this human body, we are going to have a war with this flesh.

There is, however, a unifying theme in the phrases quoted above emphasized by the word *commit*. The verb is repeatedly used in 1 John, and it teaches that a Christian will not continue in the lifestyle of sin that dominated his previous life. As a lost man, he sinned constantly without a care about that sin; as a saved man, he cannot make sin the practice of his life.

"Are we now perfect, Pastor John?" Of course not. A saved person may tell himself that he has not sinned, but he is only deluding himself. If he continually engages in sin he will discover some consequences that are unpleasant. His sin will "grieve...the holy Spirit of God" (Ephesians 4:30) resulting in personal conviction. If the sin is not dealt with, God promises to bring the chastening rod, because "whom the Lord loveth he chasteneth, and scourgeth every son whom he receiveth. If ye endure chastening, God dealeth with you as with sons; for what son is he whom the father chasteneth not? But if ye be without chastisement, whereof all are partakers, then are ye bastards, and not sons" (Hebrews 12:6–8). The chastening of a disobedient child is one of the great demonstrations of both the love of God and the fact that someone is truly saved.

John delivers a solemn warning to the Christian who will not respond to the chastisement of God. "There is a sin unto death" (1 John 5:16), a sin so serious that God acts to punish the person with physical death.[23] Notice that Pastor John did not say there was a particular sin that could be committed that would bring death. Instead, he warns the church of "all unrighteousness" (1 John 5:17) indicating that a Christian who refuses to respond to the work of God in their life will discover their Heavenly Father will resort to stronger chastisement ultimately concluding with "a sin unto death." Though God would certainly be righteous in bringing instant judgment, He is long-suffering and patient. How often He turns His wrath away!

This is the reason the child of God clings to 1 John 1:9: "If we confess our sins, he is faithful and just to forgive us our sins, and to cleanse us from all unrighteousness." Once more Pastor John was preaching to himself. No matter how long a person has been saved, he still must keep short accounts with God.

The word *confess* means "to say the same thing." When we confess our sins, we are simply agreeing with God that our sins are our responsibility and are wrong in the eyes of God. It is important to note that we must confess our "sins." In 1 John 1:8, the "claim2be" was saying he did not sin because he was not a sinner. Now, Pastor John sets the record straight by explaining that we commit sins because we are sinners. An apple tree is not an apple tree because it bears apples; it bears apples because it is an apple tree. The sins we do simply exhibit our heart condition.

When a child of God sins, however, he cannot bear the thought of offending God. He is convicted of his sin and then desires to do something about it, so he cries out to God: "I have sinned; it is wrong; it is mine." He then discovers a glorious truth about his Father: He is "faithful and just to forgive." Our God is always true to His word as "he abideth faithful: he cannot deny himself" (2 Timothy 2:13). When He forgives the repentant Christian, the Bible says He is acting out of justice.

What an astounding statement! When we consider the words *just* or *justice*, we imaging a judge punishing the guilty. We expect him to pound the gavel on the desk and protect society by demanding that payment be made for the crime, whether that payment be a fine or time in prison. The judge is *required* to punish the guilty, or he is not just.

So it is with God. His holiness demands that our sins be punished, but when we approach Him with a heart of confession, He goes to the cross. There Jesus paid the price for our sins, and there is no double jeopardy with God. Those sins cannot be paid for twice, because Jesus paid it all the first time. He forgives us because He is true to His Word. He forgives us because it is the just and right thing to do.

Jesus' blood shed at Calvary is the reason the child of God cannot dwell with unconfessed sins. When he looks at the suffering Saviour, he recognizes that he has broken the heart of his Father. The unsaved man, however, has no conviction of his sin, no desire to take the responsibility for it, nor any concern that he has offended God. The suffering of Christ does not move him.

As a young man was heading to college, his mother, who had always done his laundry, handed him a canvas duffel bag. "Put your dirty clothes in this every night," she said. "At the end of the week, wash them at the laundromat."

Seven days later, he took his dirty clothes to the laundromat, but in order to save time, he threw the entire duffel bag in the machine. He tossed some laundry soap on the bag, inserted the quarters, and started it up. Soon the entire laundromat felt the thumping of the machine. A pretty young lady approached the helpless freshman and said, "I watched you load your washer. I think the clothes would get cleaner if you took them out of the bag."[24]

Pastor John told the folk to take the sins out of the bag and confess them to the Lord. It is the antidote for a Christian who is miserable with the sin in his life. He does not want to go on until he has been cleansed, purified, and restored to his Father. He cannot be comfortable with sin in his life.

So how do we respond to sin? Does it bother us? Do we desire to be cleansed of it as quickly as possible? Are we comfortable with our sin? One of the greatest confirmations that a person is a child of God is his painful reaction to his own sin, while the lost man simply doesn't care.

3. Do I desire the Bible?

The Ephesian church members were repeatedly reminded of the importance of the Word of God as the only basis in the matter of eternal life. Pastor John continued to emphasize the Bible: "But whoso keepeth his word, in him verily is the love of God perfected: hereby know we that we are in him" (1 John 2:5). One of the best means of determining our spiritual condition is found in analyzing our attitude toward the Scriptures.

A Christian wants to know the Bible for many reasons:

- The Bible tells us how to have a life of joy (1 John 1:4).
- The Bible tells us of the character of God (1 John 1:5).
- The Bible tells us how to live victoriously over sin (1 John 2:1).
- The Bible tells us how the love of God is perfected (completed) in our lives (1 John 2:5).
- The Bible never changes (1 John 2:7).
- The Bible tells us how to overcome the enemy (1 John 2:14).
- The Bible exposes false religion (1 John 2:21).
- The Bible tells us how to believe on the Lord Jesus Christ (1 John 3:23).
- The Bible tells us how to love our brothers (1 John 4:21).
- The Bible is the witness of God (1 John 5:9).

Many religious people boast of their love for Christ with slogans, t-shirts, and bumper stickers, but Pastor John had a different idea of demonstrating our love for Christ: "For this is the love of God, that we keep his commandments" (1 John 5:3). When someone loves God, their life will display a desire to know the Bible, obey the Bible, and keep the Bible. *Keeping* His commands means that we will guard and preserve His Word. The Word of God is such a precious treasure we will literally protect it with our lives.

To the child of God the commands of the Word of God are "not grievous." He does not find Christianity to be a burdensome life full of rules and restrictions. He is more than happy to invest his life in following Christ, knowing that His "yoke is easy, and (His) burden is light" (Matthew 11:30). This does not mean that God's laws are not exacting or demanding, but rather, that God's laws are not oppressive or crushing. They are not a terrible weight we cannot bear.[25]

So there are questions to be asked regarding our relationship to the Bible: Do we desire to read the Word of God? Do we want to understand the Word of God? Do we desire to hear the Bible taught and preached? Do we find the Bible fascinating as the written Word of God? If our life is demonstrating a love and thirst for the Scriptures, we are behaving in a manner the unsaved person does not understand, and we are displaying a tremendous confirmation of the saved life. But if we have no passion for God's Word there is a serious problem.

4. Do I pass the test of time?

One of Pastor John's favorite preaching themes was abiding in Christ, a theme found forty-one times in the Book of John and twenty-six times in the three epistles of John. In 1 John 2:6, he put it like this: "He that saith he abideth in him ought himself also so to walk, even as he walked." When someone is born into the family of God, they will continue and remain in their walk with God.

One can almost hear a church member say, "Wait a minute, Pastor John. What about that fellow who came to our church a few years ago and was saved? He was on fire for God! He was a bold witness for Jesus on the job and in his family. Now, he is nowhere to be found. He is living in horrible sin and disgracing our church. What happened to him, Pastor?"

Another would add: "What about that teacher who used to tell us about Christ? He stood in the class and taught us, yet now he is following the teachings of Cerinthus. He is going everywhere convincing people that Jesus was not the Son of God! How can that be? How can someone follow the true Christ one day, and then follow the false christ the next day?"

Watch Pastor John's feeble hands reach for the Scriptures and hold the parchment before the people. "This then is the message which we have heard of him, and declare unto you" (1 John 1:5). He reminds them, "We go to the Bible as the only authority. We do not follow men's reasoning, we follow the Scriptures alone."

He then makes a stunning statement: "Little children, it is the last time: and as ye have heard that antichrist shall come, even now are there many antichrists; whereby we know that it is the last time" (1 John 2:18).

There are a lot of discussions and speculation as to who the antichrist will be during the Great Tribulation. Over the course of time, Nero, Napoleon, Hitler, Mussolini, and Gorbachev have been identified as the potential antichrist. Someone once wrote that Ronald Reagan must be the antichrist because his first, middle, and last name had six letters apiece. A Republican congressional candidate from Montana once called Hillary Clinton the antichrist.

Pastor John was far more concerned about the antichrists that were in Ephesus than the coming world leader. It is the reason he warned the church, "even now are there many antichrists." He understood that antichrists are individuals who oppose Christ and replace Christ, so he passionately promoted the true Christ while blasting the false.

He continued with the striking words: "They went out from us, but they were not of us; for if they had been of us, they would *no doubt* have continued with us: but *they went out*, that they might be made manifest that they were not all of us" (1 John 2:19). The people must have been shocked. Pastor John taught them that false teachers who denied Christ were not coming out of the houses of sin and classrooms of atheist professors, they were coming out "from us." They were once members of the congregation in Ephesus listening to John or Timothy or perhaps even Paul, but now they were preaching a false gospel.

The reason they left is because "they were not of us." Notice that Pastor John did not say, "They were of us but they lost their salvation and became antichrists." Instead, he told the church they never were of them. They may have sung the hymns, taught classes, participated in potluck dinners, gave to mission projects, helped in building programs, mowed the lawn, sung in the choir, and worked in the nursery, but they did so as *unsaved people*. It must have seemed surreal to the members, but it was so.

John goes on: "for if they had been of us, they would *no doubt* have continued with us." The word *abide* in verse six is the same word translated *continued* in verse nineteen. If a teacher was of God, he would have remained in the truth, but when a false leader is in the local church, God will ultimately expose him. *"They went out, that they might be made manifest that they were not all of us."* They may leave the church convinced they are doing so of their own accord, but the Bible says it is God who is removing them. In so doing, He is showing the church that the teacher never was of God nor of the truth. He may get away with his duplicity for a while, but God will surely make it abundantly clear that they never belonged in the first place.

Time is a powerful evaluator. It will condone a ministry or condemn it; it will confirm a man or contradict him. Jesus told his disciples, "I am the true vine, and my Father is the husbandman…abide in me, and I in you" (John 15:1, 4). As a branch cannot live separate from the tree, a child of God cannot survive apart from Christ. Time will tell.

For the person questioning their salvation, this is powerful. If you have a longing for Jesus and His Word, and that desire has remained with you, it is a powerful criterion for salvation. The pretender may look the part for a while, but God will show him for what he is. There comes a time when the unsaved man gets tired of playing the game.

Once again, there are questions and issues to raise: Do we pass the test of time? Do I still have a heart for the Bible when the months and years have slipped by? Even when I battle my flesh and sin against the Saviour, do I still continue to know the conviction of the Spirit of God? If we find ourselves abiding in Him, that is a wonderful statement of being in the vine because God promises to expose the charlatan. However, if we find that we are more comfortable on the outside looking in, and there is no conviction or heart to abide in Him, something is terribly wrong.

A study of 1 John will raise many other questions and issues, so Pastor John patiently explained how a Christian thinks, responds, and lives. These points all serve a double purpose: for either the Word of God will bring perfect assurance that a person is saved, or it will expose a man trying to get to Heaven by his own works or righteousness. Either way, the truth is a blessed thing! There is glorious peace when "we know that we are of the truth" (1 John 3:19), our hearts do not condemn us, and we have "confidence toward God" (1 John 3:22). There is great hope when the Scriptures show us "whosoever sinneth hath not seen him, neither known him" (1 John 3:6), for when a sinner is convicted of his sins, he is ready to look to the Saviour.

Mrs. Joseph Knapp, the wife of the founder of the Metropolitan Life Company, was a close friend of the famous hymn writer, Fanny Crosby. One day, she played a melody and asked Miss Crosby, "What does that tune say?"

Fanny Crosby responded, "Why, that says, blessed assurance, Jesus is mine!"

> Blessed assurance, Jesus is mine!
> O what a foretaste of glory divine!
> Heir of salvation, purchase of God,
> Born of His Spirit, washed in His blood.
>
> Perfect submission, perfect delight!
> Visions of rapture now burst on my sight;
> Angels descending bring from above
> Echoes of mercy, whispers of love.

Perfect submission—all is at rest;
I in my Saviour am happy and blest;
Watching and waiting, looking above,
Filled with His goodness, lost in His love.

This is my story, this is my song,
Praising my Saviour all the day long;
This is my story, this is my song,
Praising my Saviour all the day long.[26]

That would be the song of the ones who *know that they know*.

Chapter Six

HE DID ALL THE SAVIN'

An eight-year-old boy approached his pastor one day wanting to be baptized. The pastor had concerns as to whether the young man truly understood salvation, so he asked him to explain it. "That's easy," the boy replied. "I did my part, and Jesus did His part."

That response worried the pastor. Knowing that the Bible repeatedly says that salvation is "not of works" (Ephesians 2:9), the pastor asked him, "What do you mean when you say that you did your part and Jesus did His part?"

The fellow responded, "I did all the sinnin'. Jesus did all the savin'."

That young man has something to teach all of us. As preachers, I fear we sometimes analyze salvation until no one understands it, and our minds (our thinking) are "corrupted from the simplicity that is in Christ" (2 Corinthians 11:3). We study the book of Romans and are amazed at the dazzling depths of so great salvation, yet we can miss the point that "whosoever shall call upon the name of the Lord shall be saved" (Romans 10:13).

"I did all the sinnin'. Jesus did all the savin'."

Pastor John never forgot that he was dealing with people at different stages of their Christian life. They are described in 1 John 2:13 as fathers, young men, and little children. The *fathers* were those who had been saved for a length of time and had built a solid reputation, some of whom had even personally known Christ when He walked on earth. The *young men* were the next generation that had seen the life victories that resulted from their desire for and obedience to the Bible.

Little children was John's term of affection for the entire church. Whether someone was a seasoned saint or just beginning their walk, the old preacher loved them like they were his own. It is fascinating to read 1 John 2:13–14 and listen to the pastor repeat himself. With the shift in the verb tenses we can almost hear him say: "I told you before how you stand with God, and I am telling you again. Things have not changed with you or with God!"

Pastor John wanted his "little children" to *know that they know,* so he was never too busy to drive home the same old truth: we do all the sinning, but Jesus does all the saving. There is a popular strain of religion that convinces people that Jesus may have done the saving in the past, but we must work to keep ourselves saved in the present. One of the largest denominations in America, the Assemblies of God, believes "it is possible for a person once saved to turn from God and be lost again."[27] Pastor John consistently taught a different message.

When someone in the Ephesian church began to doubt their spiritual condition, we can hear John remind them: "And this is the promise that he hath promised us, even eternal life" (1 John 2:25). He told them, "let that therefore abide in you, which ye have heard from the beginning" (1 John 2:24). This is why God's men are commanded to preach the Word of God, for when the Bible is taught, and a child of God continues in it, they begin to grasp the life-changing truth that eternal life is promised by God.

Once again, John gets back to the authority of the Bible. At the moment of conversion when someone becomes a Christian, they must understand what the Scriptures say about salvation. Then the old truths of the Bible must be constantly reinforced so they will abide in the life of the believer. Three times in that single verse Pastor John uses the word for abiding because the Bible must find a permanent home in our minds if we will continue for Him.

When the Bible rests in the soul and the mind of the child of God, he begins to appreciate that eternal life is a promise. When someone would ask him, "So Pastor John, how do you know that you have eternal life?" The old preacher would smile and say, "God promised me." Pastor John knew that if he could lose eternal life, then it was never eternal to begin with, and God would be the liar.

Hudson Taylor, the faithful missionary to China, was going through a trying time. He once wrote this in a letter to his wife: "We have twenty-five cents and all the promises of God!"

He certainly was a wealthy man!

By clinging to the Bible, we become confident and convinced. How do I know I am saved? God promised me! How do I know I am going to Heaven? God promised me! How do I know I am ready to die? God promised me!

Pastor John had a few more promises from God for his people:

- God promised to wash away all my sin (1 John 1:7).
- God promised to take away (destroy) my sin (1 John 3:5).
- God promised to assure my heart (1 John 3:19).

- God promised to give me the Holy Spirit
  (1 John 3:24).
- God promised to make me bold in the day of
  judgment (1 John 4:17).
- God promised to give me eternal life (1 John 5:11).

Notice that it is God that does all the work! We do not save ourselves, nor do we keep ourselves saved.

If that weren't enough, Pastor John preached this: "Beloved, now are we the sons of God" (1 John 3:2). The Bible does not say that one day in the future—if we work hard and keep ourselves saved—we will become the sons of God. Instead, the very moment sinners receive Jesus Christ as Saviour, they "become the sons of God" (John 1:12). Meditate on that for a moment. Right now I am a child of God. Right now I am in the family of God.

"I did all the sinnin'. Jesus did all the savin'."

A farmer who lacked the assurance of salvation once foolishly prayed that as an evidence of his acceptance, the Lord would cause ten sheep of his flock—and only ten—to gather in a certain shed out in the pasture. Later that day, when the farmer anxiously approached the shed, he was relieved to find exactly ten sheep. That gave him a temporary sense of peace, but soon doubt returned with the shocking thought that it may have been just a coincidence. So he asked the Lord that ten different sheep might gather in an opposite corner of the pasture. And they did!

When the farmer was asked, "Did this give you assurance?" he said, "No, nothing gave me certainty until I got the sure Word of God for it."[28]

When we finally grasp the fact that Jesus is eternal life, we are at the place of victory. He did everything in the past, He does everything today, and He will do everything tomorrow. Salvation is not up to us; it is up to Him. As the promises of God rest in our souls, we stop trying to arrange the sheep in the shed and simply take Him at His word.

Then, we *know that we know.*

Chapter Seven

BECAUSE GOD SAID SO

It would be easy to imagine an Ephesian church member sitting in the office with Pastor John. He is struggling with assurance of his salvation, and, more than anything in the world, he wants to *know that he knows.* "Pastor, my problem is my sin. I worry that God cannot forgive me. In past days, I did some mighty embarrassing things; and even now when I sin, I begin to think I cannot be saved. If I am a child of God, why do I sin?"

Perhaps such a conversation motivated the burdened man of God to plead with the people: "My little children, these things write I unto you, that ye sin not" (1 John 2:1). What a personal message. It was the first of nine occasions in 1 John where he displayed his intense concern for the people he loved by using the word *I*. Some of his little children were getting too close to the world; others were losing their love for Christ and each other. He could see some folks meandering towards shipwreck, and it broke his heart.

At the conclusion of the first chapter of 1 John the preacher was dealing with self righteous people who convinced themselves they were not capable of sinning. But now, the attention turns to his beloved children that were broken over their sins. Immediately, he gives them a message of hope with these words: "*if* any man sin." He is telling them, "We do not *have* to sin. We *can* live in victory. It is not a foregone conclusion that sin will master us."

What hope! The Bible says it is possible for a Christian to have victory and choose not to sin. The commentator John Phillips put it like this: "It would be an error to say that a believer *is not able* to sin. Romans 7 and all Christian experience prove that to be false. It would be true to say, however, that a believer is *able not* to sin."[29]

John brings them into the "courtroom of the skies." Using terms found in the legal profession, he wants his beloved children to know what happened to their sins the instant they were saved. We cannot *know that we know* until we comprehend what God has done with our sins.

We stand before the Judge of the "quick and the dead" (1 Peter 4:5) in woeful condition. Before a witness takes the stand, before a word of defense is spoken, before a single cross examination is heard, the outcome of this trial is assured for we are "condemned already" (John 3:18). "As by one man sin entered into the world, and death by sin; and so death passed upon all men, for that all have sinned" (Romans 5:12). This trial is over before it starts.

To make matters worse, we are not judged by human standards or witness, but by the Bible. "The word that I have spoken, the same shall judge him in the last day" (John 12:48). When that Word is opened, it paints an ugly picture:

As it is written, there is none righteous, no, not
one: There is none that understandeth, there is
none that seeketh after God. They are all gone out
of the way, they are together become unprofitable;
there is none that doeth good, no, not one. Their
throat is an open sepulchre; with their tongues
they have used deceit; the poison of asps is under
their lips: Whose mouth is full of cursing and
bitterness: Their feet are swift to shed blood:
Destruction and misery are in their ways: And the
way of peace have they not known: There is no
fear of God before their eyes.—ROMANS 3:10–18

God has exposed us for what we really are. He
knows that our minds are evil, our tongues are evil,
our lips are evil, our mouths are evil, our feet are evil,
and our eyes are evil. He looks into our hearts and
finds an open tomb full of death.

There is absolutely no place for us to hide. "Am
I a God at hand, saith the LORD, and not a God afar
off? Can any hide himself in secret places that I shall
not see him? saith the LORD. Do not I fill heaven and
earth? saith the LORD" (Jeremiah 23:23–24). Nowhere
to go. No word to speak. No ploy to use. We can only

grimly take a seat and wait for the verdict. When it comes, it will sound like this: "Depart from me, ye cursed, into everlasting fire" (Matthew 25:41).

It is then we realize that someone has come along side of us. It is astounding to think that anyone would be associated with a case so helpless and hopeless, yet there He is. We ask Him why He is standing there, and He responds by pointing to 1 John 2:1: "If any man sin, we have an advocate." He explains that an advocate is our representative "with the Father," meaning that He will stand for us, speak for us, and approach the judge for us. When we remind Him how defenseless we are, He reminds us how perfect He is. "I am Jesus Christ the righteous." He not only *does* what is right, He *is* right, for He "did no sin, neither was guile found in his mouth" (1 Peter 2:22). He is well able to stand in the holy courtroom of Heaven on our behalf.

We have to wonder how we are going to pay the bill, but He explains that payment has already been rendered. "Ho, every one that thirsteth, come ye to the waters, and he that hath no money; come ye, buy, and eat; yea, come, buy wine and milk without money and without price" (Isaiah 55:1). There is no charge; in fact, He actually paid for the privilege of defending us!

For the first time there is hope. We are being defended by an advocate that has never lost a case. He will know what to do. He will know what to say.

As we watch Him approach the bench, we convince ourselves that He knows how to maneuver in this courtroom. Perhaps He knows an expert witness who will testify that we are not responsible for our sins. Perhaps He will parse verbs and find a technicality for us to be set free. He will find a way.

But when He approaches the bench, He does not offer a plea bargain, nor does He attempt to find a legal loophole. He simply says, "Your Honor, my client is guilty." We are stunned at such an admission, yet there is nothing else He can say. The book says: "Now we know that what things soever the law saith, it saith to them who are under the law: that every mouth may be stopped, and all the world may become guilty before God" (Romans 3:19). The book says: "For whosoever shall keep the whole law, and yet offend in one point, he is guilty of all" (James 2:10).

Guilty. Condemned. Lost.

We can only ask our advocate, "Is there any hope for a sinner?" He explains that our only possibility of escaping the judgment to come would be to find a *propitiation*, one who takes the punishment another deserves. He explains that the propitiation must be approved by the judge, for he must satisfy the wrath of the judge. "Where can we find such a propitiation?" He points to 1 John 2:2: "And he is the propitiation for our sins: and not for ours only, but also for the sins of the whole world."

Our sins cannot simply be covered up. Our sins cannot be ignored. Our sins cannot be swept under the rug. Our sins must be paid for.

When the prophet Isaiah looked through the telescope of prophecy to Calvary, he wrote of God's perspective: "He shall see of the travail of his soul, and shall be satisfied: by his knowledge shall my righteous servant justify many; for he shall bear their iniquities" (Isaiah 53:11). When the Father saw His only begotten Son on the cross, He put His stamp of approval on the sacrifice, and Jesus was accepted as the propitiation.

No priest is needed. No religion is needed. No penance is needed. Jesus is "the way, the truth, and the life" (John 14:6). Nothing less. Nothing more. No one else.

Pastor John goes on to explain the simplicity of salvation with these verses:

> In this was manifested the love of God toward us, because that God sent his only begotten Son into the world, that we might live through him. Herein is love, not that we loved God, but that he loved us, and sent his Son to be the propitiation for our sins.—1 JOHN 4:9–10

> These things have I written unto you that believe on the name of the Son of God; that ye may know that ye have eternal life, and that ye may believe on the name of the Son of God. —1 JOHN 5:13

> And we have seen and do testify that the Father sent the Son to be the Saviour of the world. Whosoever shall confess that Jesus is the Son of God, God dwelleth in him, and he in God. —1 JOHN 4:14–15

When it comes to salvation, God says it is "manifested…toward us." Most people think it is impossible to know for sure that they are going to Heaven. They hope so, think so, pray so, but at the end of the day, no one can know for sure. But God has a different point of view. He made salvation so plain and clear even a child can grasp it. It is His intent that every human see it, understand it, and believe it.

Yet again, it is emphasized that the only source for salvation is the Word of God. Pastor John could say, "We have seen and do testify." The old man of God was still preaching the same message six decades later, and that witness and testimony is right before us in the Bible.

God's salvation is in the person of the Son of God, Jesus Christ. In the five verses quoted above there are seven references to Jesus Christ. Every verse in the Bible that explains salvation will have a reference to Jesus because He *is* salvation.

Note again that "we do all the sinnin'. He does all the savin.'" When it comes to biblical salvation, it is the work of God that saves and not our human efforts. It was God who sent His Son into the world. It was God who "first loved us" (1 John 4:19). It was God who gave His Son to be the propitiation. It was God who sent His Son to be the "Saviour of the world."

A sinner is saved by believing on Jesus and confessing that He is the Son of God. In our hearts, we are trusting Him and not ourselves. With our tongues, we confess that He is the Saviour sent by God. This is beautifully described in Romans 10:9–10: "That if thou shalt confess with thy mouth the Lord Jesus, and shalt believe in thine heart that God hath raised him from the dead, thou shalt be saved. For with the heart man believeth unto righteousness; and with the mouth confession is made unto salvation."

Some have nitpicked as to which is first—the confession or the belief. The Bible says they are simultaneous. One verse says confess and believe. The next verse says believe and confess. Our mouth speaks what our heart believes: "I am not trusting in my religion. I am not trusting my goodness, for I have none. I am not trusting in my own way. I am trusting

Jesus and only Jesus as my Saviour. He died. He rose again. He is my only hope."

Suddenly the great trial in the skies takes on a changed perspective. With Jesus as our Saviour, we "have boldness in the day of judgment" (1 John 4:17). That boldness is not an arrogant self-confidence, but rather a strength and courage we have because of what Jesus has done for us. We watch our Advocate approach the bench:

"Your Honor, my client has trusted me to be the propitiation. He has confessed with his tongue the belief in his heart."

The booming voice of the Judge fills the courtroom: "What has washed his sins away?" All eyes in the courtroom go to the Bible which is opened to 1 John 1:7: "The blood of Jesus Christ his Son cleanseth us from all sin!"

The Judge has a one word response. "Justified!"

The Judge has declared us to be righteous because Jesus is righteous. It is not that He ignores our sins. It is not that He dismisses our sins. Instead, He sees us through the sacrifice of His Son on the cross and the blood that He shed. "Much more then, being now justified by his blood, we shall be saved from wrath through him" (Romans 5:9).

From our Sunday School days, we have been told that to be *justified* means "just as if we have never sinned," but actually, it is more than that. Justification means that God is declaring me to be in right standing with Him because of Jesus. It means that I now have the righteousness of Christ.

Justification is the heart of the issue. It is the key if someone wants to *know that they know.* Our doubts and confusion cause us to question how a person can truly be saved who has committed such horrible sins. Yet the answer could not be more complete. When a sinner "believes" and "confesses" Christ, the sins are completely washed away by the precious blood of Jesus. We no longer have our "own righteousness, which is of the law, but that which is through the faith of Christ, the righteousness which is of God by faith" (Philippians 3:9).

When we dive into the Word of God, we discover an abundance of verses that reaffirm the promise of

1 John 1:7. Look what happened to our sins the instant we trusted Christ:

- John 1:29—He takes our sins away.
- Jeremiah 50:20—He puts them in a place where they will not be found.
- Micah 7:19—He casts them into the sea.
- Isaiah 1:18—He makes our sins as white as snow; He makes our sins as wool.
- Isaiah 38:17—He casts them behind His back.
- Isaiah 43:25—He blots them out.
- Isaiah 44:22—He makes them disappear like a morning mist (cloud).
- Jeremiah 31:34—He remembers them no more.
- Exodus 34:7—He forgives iniquities, transgressions, and sin.
- Psalm 32:1—He covers our sin.
- Psalm 103:12—He removes them as far as the east is from the west.

And for good measure, look what He did the moment we called out to Him:

- Acts 13:39—He justifies our sins.

- Romans 4:8—He does not impute our sins.
- Ephesians 1:7—He forgives our sins.
- Hebrews 1:3—He purges our sins.
- 1 John 1:7—He cleanses us from all sin.
- Revelation 1:5—He washes us from our sins.
- Luke 1:77—He remits our sins.
- Jeremiah 33:8—He pardons us.
- Psalm 130:8—He redeems us from all iniquities.

Suddenly our frail human doubts look mighty petty. We stack the promises of God against our failed thinking, and we are overwhelmed by His grace. When I doubt God's salvation, I am calling into question promise after promise that He has made. How else could God state it? What other illustration can He give to explain it?

My sins are long gone. How do I know they are gone?

Because God said so!

An old time preacher from Minneapolis had finished his message on the text "Quench not the Spirit." When he stepped down from the pulpit, a

young man from a godless family was on the front row
in "great agony of the soul." The pastor first pointed
him to the Scriptures and the glorious truth that
Christ had borne all his sins on the cross, then gave
him the precious invitation to come to Christ and be
saved. They young man said, "I have accepted Christ,
but I cannot believe my sins are gone." He left the
building in distress.

The next evening, the young man returned to
the preaching service where the preacher opened
the Bible to John 3:36: "He that believeth on the Son
hath everlasting life." He said, "Hector, who does God
here say hath everlasting life?" He answered, "He that
believeth on the Son."

The conversation went back and forth: "Do you
believe on the Son?"

"I do."

"What does God say?"

"He that believeth on the Son hath everlasting life."

"What have you?"

"Oh, won't you pray for me?"

"Yes, I will pray for you," and the preacher went over it again.

"He that believeth on the Son hath everlasting life." "Who has everlasting life?"

"He that believeth on the Son."

"How many that believe on the Son have everlasting life?"

"Everyone."

"Have you believed on the Son?"

"I have."

"What does God say about those who believe on the Son?"

"They have everlasting life."

"Are you sure that they that believe on the Son have everlasting life?"

"I am sure."

"What makes you so sure?"

"God says so."

"What does God say?"

"He that believeth on the Son hath everlasting life."

"Do you believe on the Son?"

"I do."

"What does God say you have?"

"Oh, will you pray for me?"

The preacher went over it again and again, but the young man could not seem to grasp it. At last he arose and started slowly down the aisle to leave the building asking the pastor, "Will you pray for me?" He said, "I will."

He let him get part way down the aisle and then called after him, "Hector, do you believe that I will pray for you?"

"Why, I know you will," he replied.

"How do you know that I will?"

"Because you said so."

"Is not God's word as good as mine?"

The truth flashed upon Hector's soul in a moment. He saw that while he had been ready to believe the preacher, he had not been ready to believe God. He took God at His Word and knew he had everlasting life *because God said so* and went home rejoicing in perfect assurance that his sins were all forgiven.[30]

There are many reasons we can know we have eternal life. But for all the illustrations, arguments, persuasions, analysis, expositions, sermons, quips, and stories, there is one reason that tops them all.

God said so.

That is why we *know that we know.*

Chapter Eight

NINETEEN WORDS

"But, Pastor John!" One can almost hear the wavering church member raise the issue of assurance yet again. It is heartbreaking to deal with someone struggling with their salvation as they repeatedly ask the same questions, make the same points, but never seem to get the answer. When a patient pastor like the Apostle John carefully explains the Bible solution, it often seems as if they never hear.

What is so hard about "God said so"?

There are many deep portions of the Word of God that are so profound the mightiest minds have never grasped them. Some discussions about Bible texts fuel endless debates at the conclusion of which people can only disagree. As would be expected from a book that is the very words of God, we humans often shrug our shoulders and accept the fact that God's thoughts are higher than our thoughts (Isaiah 55:9). But when it comes to God's salvation, notice how straightforward Pastor John made it:

> The blood of Jesus Christ his Son cleanseth us from all sin.—1 JOHN 1:9

> I write unto you, little children, because your sins are forgiven you for his name's sake.—1 JOHN 2:12

> And this is the promise that he hath promised us, even eternal life.—1 JOHN 2:25

> Beloved, now are we the sons of God.—1 JOHN 3:2

> Whosoever shall confess that Jesus is the Son of God, God dwelleth in him, and he in God. —1 JOHN 4:15

"But Pastor John!" So the venerable old man gives it one last try. He is going to make it so plain and lucid that a little child can get it:

> He that hath the Son hath life; and he that hath not the Son of God hath not life.—1 JOHN 5:12

Nineteen words. Every one of the words in our English language is but one syllable, words which could easily appear in a first grade reader for boys and girls. If you have Jesus, you have life; and if you don't have Jesus, you don't have life.

It settles all the doubts. It does not matter if a person has a religion or a church; it only matters that they have Christ. For all of the prayers and penance and giving and altar calls and sacraments, it boils down to this: either we have Jesus or we don't. Nineteen words.

Notice the verbs are in the present tense. It does not say that one day we will have Jesus, but rather, *right now* we have Him. It does not say that one day we will have eternal life, but rather, *right now* we have it. Follow the simplicity of salvation in the book of 1 John:

I believe on Christ. I confess Christ. I am born into the family of God. I am now a son of God. God dwells in me. I dwell in God. I have eternal life.

What is there to doubt?

If someone possesses *eternal life* today and they were to someday, somehow, wind up in Hell, then they do not truly possess *eternal life.* If it is eternal, then it cannot be taken away. In the New Testament, God is eternal (Romans 16:26), the Holy Spirit is eternal (Hebrews 9:14), and the kingdom of Jesus is eternal (2 Peter 1:11).[31] If my "eternal life" does not actually last forever, then the Father, the Son, and the Holy Spirit do not last forever.

As you read the book of 1 John it may be the Word of God is exposing your lost condition. You may have spent your life following a religion, trying your best, and doing a series of works to impress God, but if you have been attempting to find your own way to Heaven or have placed your confidence in anything other than the shed blood of Jesus Christ and the Word of

God, then these nineteen words need to arrest your attention. Now is the time to believe on the Christ of the Bible as your only Saviour, because irrespective of what you have done in your religious life, if you do not have Christ, you do not have life.

For someone else, the Scriptures may well be confirming "now are we the sons of God" (1 John 3:2). It is a glorious day when a child of God sees it from the Bible and gets it settled. "Today, tomorrow, and for all eternity, I am now and shall always be a child of God! I have the Son of God!"

Nineteen words.

Late in the evening of April 14, 1912, the RMS *Titanic* collided with an iceberg some 375 miles off the coast of Newfoundland. In less than three hours, the ship broke apart and foundered, taking the lives of 1,517 passengers. Two hours later, the RMS *Carpathia* arrived on the scene to rescue more than 700 others.

Crowds gathered in Liverpool, England, before the offices of the White Star Lines, the company that owned the *Titanic*. Two large boards were placed by the main entrance. On one sign were printed the words: "KNOWN TO BE SAVED." The other said: "KNOWN TO BE LOST."

Relatives and friends of the passengers waited outside of the offices for news. When it came, the name was printed on a piece of cardboard, and an employee stood before the gathered throng. A deathly silence fell upon the crowd as the name was shown to all. It was then placed either on the board of those known to be saved or on the board of those known to be lost.[32]

The *Titanic* sailed with three classes of passengers. On board were famous and wealthy people along with a host of unknown and common people. But when the ship sank, the only thing that mattered was on which board the name would be posted.

So it is with God. For all of the games we humans play and all the treasures and toys we try to amass, at the end of a life only one thing will matter: How do we stand with God?

Nineteen words say it all. Either we have Jesus and we have life, or we do not have Jesus and we do not have life. It is one or the other. If you do not have Jesus then you need to believe on the Christ of the Bible and trust Him to wash your sins away and save you. If you have believed and confessed the Christ of 1 John 5:12, the Word of God unconditionally states that you have Christ, and you should live in confidence as a child of God.

Get those nineteen words settled, and you will *know that you know.*

Notes

1. Joseph Demakis, quoting John Barrymore in *The Ultimate Book of Quotations* (Lulu Enterprises, Inc., 2012), 83.

2. The book of 1 John is unusual in that the author and recipients are not identified. There is no question that the Apostle John was the human writer by all but the most extreme liberal theologians. It is certain that John was close to the Christians to whom he wrote and that he was known by them. The known practice of John

was to write to local churches (Revelation 1:4) as they are the pillar and ground of the truth (1 Timothy 3:15). There is a host of eye witnesses who put John in the city of Ephesus in his later years as pastor of the Ephesian church. I have taken the position that Pastor John sent this letter during his labors in the church, writing to not only to the people he loved and served intimately, but also to the churches of Asia Minor where he had invested his life (Revelation 2–3). Ultimately, the book of 1 John, as well as the other sixty-five books of the Bible, are written for and are profitable to those in every generation and in every location—including us.

3. William Stuart McBirnie, *The Search for the Twelve Apostles* (Tyndale Momentum, 1665-1668), Kindle Edition.

4. J. V. McGee, *Thru the Bible commentary: The Epistles (1 John)*, (Thomas Nelson, 1991), electronic ed., Vol. 56.

5. P. L. Tan, *Encyclopedia of 7700 Illustrations: Signs of the Times* (Bible Communications, Inc., 1996).

6. R. J. Morgan, *Nelson's Complete Book of Stories, Illustrations, and Quotes* (Thomas Nelson Publishers, 2000), electronic ed., 637.

7. The verb tense is a perfect verb; a word that indicates a continuing result of a past act.

8. David Jackman,*The Message of John's Letters: Living in the Love of God* (InterVarsity Press, 1988), 36.

9. J. P. Louw & Eugene Albert Nida, Greek-English Lexicon of the New Testament: Based on Semantic Domains (United Bible Societies, 1996).

10. The word occurs forty-one times in the Gospel of John and twenty-six times in the epistles of John.

11. 1 Thessalonians 5:26; Galatians 1:2; 1 Corinthians 5:1; Romans 16:14; 1 Timothy 6:2; James 1:9; 1 Peter 5:12; 3 John 3, 5, 10.

12. J. P. Louw & Eugene Albert Nida, Greek-English Lexicon of the New Testament: Based on Semantic Domains (United Bible Societies, 1996).

13. G. W. Derickson, *First, Second, and Third John*, ed. H. W. House, W. H. Harris III, & A. W. Pitts (Logos Bible Software, 2012).

14. Rochunga Pudaite, *The Book That Set My People Free* (Tyndale House Publishers Inc., 1982), 10–13.

15. P. L. Tan, *Encyclopedia of 7700 Illustrations: Signs of the Times.* (Bible Communications, Inc.,1996).

16. There are numerous Old Testament Scriptures naming God as the Holy One (Psalm 71:22; Habakkuk 3:3; Isaiah 1:4, etc.). Jesus is also referred to as the "Holy One of God" (Mark 1:24).

17. J. P. Louw & Eugene Albert Nida, Greek-English Lexicon of the New Testament: Based on Semantic Domains (United Bible Societies, 1996).

18. J. M. Boice, *Romans: The New Humanity* (Baker Book House, 1991), Vol. 4,1820.

19. Roe Fulkerson, "He Ain't Heavy, He's My Brother," Kiwanis Magazine, September 1924.

20. 1 John 2:28; 1 John 3:21; 1 John 4:17; 1 John 5:14.

21. G. W. Derickson, *First, Second, and Third John*, ed. H. W. House, W. H. Harris III, & A. W. Pitts, (Logos Bible Software, 2012), 1 John 5:14.

22. J. P. Louw & Eugene Albert Nida, Greek-English Lexicon of the New Testament: Based on Semantic Domains (United Bible Societies, 1996).

23. G. W. Derickson, *First, Second, and Third John*, ed. H. W. House, W. H. Harris III, & A. W. Pitts (Logos Bible Software, 2012), 1 John 5:16.

24. Craig Brian Larson & Phyllis Ten Elshof, *1001 Illustrations That Connect* (Zondervan, 2009), 141.

25. D. L. Akin, *1, 2, 3 John* (Broadman & Holman Publishers, 2001), Vol. 38, 191.

26. Kenneth W. Osbeck, Amazing Grace: 366 Inspiring Hymn Stories for Daily Devotions (Kregel Publications, 1990, 2002), 327.

27. Assemblies of God doctrinal position (Accessed May, 2015), http://ag.org/top/Beliefs/topics/gendoct_09_security.cfm.

28. Galaxie Software, *10,000 Sermon Illustrations* (Biblical Studies Press, 2002).

29. John Phillips, *Exploring the Epistles of John* (Kregel Publications, 2003), 40.

30. R.A. Torrey, *Anecdotes and Illustrations* (Fleming H. Revell Company, 1907), 153–155.

31. Gerhard Kittel, G. W. Bromiley & Gerhard Friedrich, *Theological Dictionary of the New Testament* (Eerdmans, 1964).

32. Moody Adams, *The Titanic's Last Hero* (Olive Press), 23.

About the Author

PAUL SCHWANKE was saved as a young boy and soon afterward surrendered to preach the Word of God. As a teenager, he was already busy preaching in missions, youth meetings, and churches. The Lord used his early involvement to direct him to the ministry of local church evangelism. Since 1983, Evangelist Schwanke has been used of God to preach in churches across America and around the world. You can connect with him through his website, preachthebible.com.

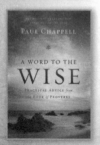

Visit us online

strivingtogether.com

wcbc.edu